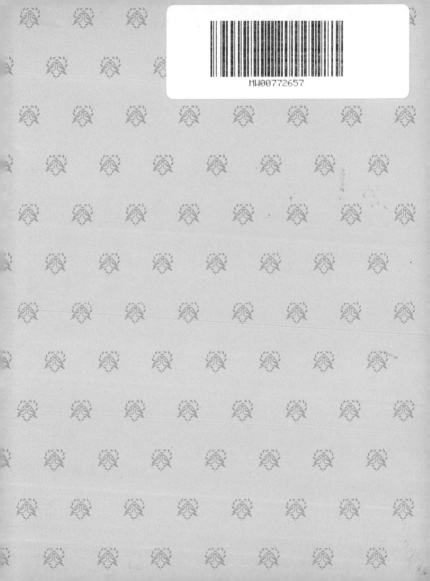

✳ L O V E   S I G N S ✳

AQUARIUS

January 21 – February 18

JULIA & DEREK PARKER

♥ ♥

📖 DK

Dedicated to Martin Lethbridge

A DK PUBLISHING BOOK

Project Editor • Annabel Morgan
Art Editor • Anna Benjamin
Managing Editor • Francis Ritter
Managing Art Editor • Derek Coombes
DTP Designer • Cressida Joyce
Production Controller • Martin Croshaw
US Editor • Constance M. Robinson

ACKNOWLEDGMENTS

Photography: Steve Gorton: pp. 10, 13–15, 17–19, 46–49; Ian O'Leary: 16. *Additional photography by:* Colin Keates, David King, Monique Le Luhandre, David Murray, Tim Ridley, Clive Streeter, Harry Taylor, Matthew Ward. *Artworks:* Nic Demin: 34–45; Peter Lawman: *jacket,* 4, 12; Paul Redgrave: 24–33; Satwinder Sehmi: *glyphs;* Jane Thomson: *borders;* Rosemary Woods: 11.

Peter Lawman's paintings are exhibited by the Portal Gallery Ltd, London.

Picture credits: Bridgeman Art Library/Hermitage, St. Petersburg: 51; Robert Harding Picture Library: 201, 20c, 20r; Images Colour Library: 9; The National Gallery, London: 11; Tony Stone Images: 21t, 21b; The Victoria and Albert Museum, London: 5; Zefa: 21c.

First American Edition, 1996
2 4 6 8 10 9 7 5 3 1

Published in the United States by
DK Publishing, Inc., 95 Madison Avenue, New York, New York 10016
Visit us on the World Wide Web at http://www.dk.com

A catalog record is available from the Library of Congress.

ISBN 0-7894-1087-7

Reproduced by Bright Arts, Hong Kong
Printed and bound by Imago, Hong Kong

CONTENTS

ASTROLOGY & YOU

THERE IS MUCH MORE TO ASTROLOGY THAN YOUR SUN SIGN.
A SIMPLE INVESTIGATION INTO THE POSITION OF THE OTHER
PLANETS AT THE MOMENT OF YOUR BIRTH WILL PROVIDE YOU
WITH FASCINATING INSIGHTS INTO YOUR PERSONALITY.

*Y*our birth sign, or Sun sign, is the sign of the zodiac that the Sun occupied at the moment of your birth. The majority of books on astrology concentrate only on explaining the relevance of the Sun signs. This is a simple form of astrology that can provide you with some interesting but rather general information about you and your personality. In this book, we take you a step further, and reveal how the planets Venus and Mars work in association with your Sun sign to influence your attitudes toward romance and sexuality.

In order to gain a detailed insight into your personality, a "natal" horoscope, or birth chart, is necessary. This details the position of all the planets in our solar system at the moment of your birth, not just the position of the Sun. Just as the Sun occupied one of the 12 zodiac signs when you were born, perhaps making you "a Geminian" or "a Sagittarian," so each of the other planets occupied a certain sign. Each planet governs a different area of your personality, and the planets Venus and Mars are responsible for your attitudes toward love and sex, respectively.

For example, if you are a Sun-sign Sagittarian, according to the attributes of the sign you should be a dynamic, freedom-loving character. However, if Venus occupied Libra when you were born, you may make a passive and clinging partner – qualities that are supposedly completely alien to Sagittarians.

A MAP OF THE CONSTELLATION

The 16th-century astronomer Copernicus first made the revolutionary suggestion that the planets orbit the Sun rather than Earth. In this 17th-century constellation chart, the Sun is shown at the center of the solar system.

The tables on pages 52–61 of this book will enable you to discover the positions of Mars and Venus at the moment of your birth. Once you have read this information, turn to pages 22–45. On these pages we explain how the influences of Venus and Mars interact with the characteristics of your Sun sign. This information will provide you with many illuminating insights into your personality, and explains how the planets have formed your attitudes toward love and sex.

LOOKING FOR A LOVER

ASTROLOGY CAN PROVIDE YOU WITH VALUABLE INFORMATION
ON HOW TO INITIATE AND MAINTAIN RELATIONSHIPS. IT CAN
ALSO TELL YOU HOW COMPATIBLE YOU ARE WITH YOUR LOVER,
AND HOW SUCCESSFUL YOUR RELATIONSHIP IS LIKELY TO BE.

*P*eople frequently use astrology to lead into a relationship, and "What sign are you?" is often used as a conversation opener. Some people simply introduce the subject as an opening gambit, while others place great importance on this question and its answer.

Astrology can affect the way you think and behave when you are in love. It can also provide you with fascinating information about your lovers and your relationships. Astrology cannot tell you who to fall in love with or who to avoid, but it can offer you some very helpful advice.

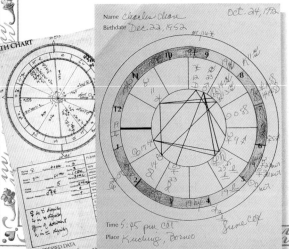

BIRTH CHARTS
Synastry involves the comparison of two people's charts in order to assess their compatibility in all areas of their relationship. The process can highlight any areas of common interest or potential conflict.

THE TABLE OF ELEMENTS

People whose signs are grouped under the same element tend to find it easy to fall into a happy relationship. The groupings are:

FIRE: *Aries, Leo, Sagittarius*
EARTH: *Taurus, Virgo, Capricorn*
AIR: *Gemini, Libra, Aquarius*
WATER: *Cancer, Scorpio, Pisces*

When you meet someone to whom you are attracted, astrology can provide you with a valuable insight into his or her personality. It may even reveal unattractive characteristics that your prospective partner is trying to conceal.

Astrologers are often asked to advise lovers involved in an ongoing relationship, or people who are contemplating a love affair. This important aspect of astrology is called synastry, and involves comparing the birth charts of the two people concerned. Each birth chart records the exact position of the planets at the moment and place of a person's birth.

By interpreting each chart separately, then comparing them, an astrologer can assess the compatibility of any two people, showing where problems may arise in their relationship, and where strong bonds will form.

One of the greatest astrological myths is that people of some signs are not compatible with people of certain other signs. This is completely untrue. Whatever your Sun sign, you can have a happy relationship with a person of any other sign.

YOU & YOUR LOVER

KNOWING ABOUT YOURSELF AND YOUR LOVER IS THE KEY TO
A HAPPY RELATIONSHIP. HERE WE REVEAL THE TRADITIONAL
ASSOCIATIONS OF AQUARIUS, YOUR COMPATIBILITY WITH ALL THE
SUN SIGNS, AND THE FLOWERS LINKED WITH EACH SIGN.

ALL FRUIT TREES,
INCLUDING THE
CHERRY TREE, ARE
LINKED WITH
AQUARIUS

AQUAMARINE IS
THE AQUARIAN
BIRTHSTONE

AQUARIUS IS
RULED BY THE
PLANET URANUS

ELECTRIC BLUE
AND BRIGHT
TURQUOISE ARE
THE COLORS
OF AQUARIUS

AQUARIUS IS
THE SIGN OF
THE WATER-
POURER, AND
PERSONIFICATIONS
OF THIS SIGN ARE
ALWAYS SHOWN
WITH AN URN
OF WATER

A DIGNIFIED,
ERECT STANCE IS
CHARACTERISTIC
OF AQUARIANS

AQUARIUS RULES BIRDS
CAPABLE OF LONG-
DISTANCE FLIGHT

AQUARIUS AND ARIES
This is an adventurous and enterprising combination. You have many similarities – you are both forward-looking, honest, and independent. This is potentially a true marriage of minds.

Lavender is a Geminian flower

Thistles are ruled by Aries

AQUARIUS AND GEMINI
Geminian flirtatiousness will not bother you, because you are not the jealous type. You possess a strong intellectual rapport, and will both enjoy stimulating debates and discussions.

AQUARIUS AND TAURUS
Warmhearted Taureans may be confused by your air of detachment, and you will find Taurean possessiveness hard to bear. You must both work hard to overcome your differences.

The lily, and other white flowers, are ruled by Cancer

The rose is associated with Taurus

AQUARIUS AND CANCER
Cancerians yearn for domestic security, and are very dependent on their partners. Your cool self-sufficiency will make them feel insecure. You must work hard to make this alliance succeed.

AQUARIUS AND LEO

This could be an excellent union. Leo will warm your cool heart, and your Aquarian honesty will deflate any leonine pretensions or pomposity. You will be a bold and adventurous couple.

Hydrangeas are governed by Libra

Sunflowers are ruled by Leo

AQUARIUS AND LIBRA

Conventional Librans may be embarrassed by your eccentricity. However, Librans make loving, and supportive partners, and their sense of romance will melt even your cool heart.

AQUARIUS AND VIRGO

Self-sufficient Virgos will not threaten your independence, and they will admire your honesty and idealism. The two of you will form a stimulating, long-lasting, and loving relationship.

Honeysuckle is attributed to Scorpio

AQUARIUS AND SCORPIO

The intensity of Scorpio emotion will be irritating to detached Aquarians, while they will think you are rather cold. You will both have to work very hard to make this alliance succeed.

Small, brightly colored flowers are associated with Virgo

AQUARIUS AND SAGITTARIUS
You are both independent and honest, and should develop an excellent understanding. A fiery Sagittarian will warm you up, but will not be overintense or clinging. A perfect partnership.

Orchids are associated with Aquarius

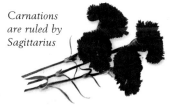

Carnations are ruled by Sagittarius

AQUARIUS AND AQUARIUS
You understand each other perfectly. The Aquarian romantic streak will be revealed, and you will share many interests and enthusiasms. Your sex life should be adventurous and exciting.

AQUARIUS AND CAPRICORN
Capricorn and Aquarius have much in common. You will relish the wit and intelligence of Capricorns, but their conformity may clash with your eccentric and unconventional lifestyle.

Viburnum is governed by Pisces

Pansies are Capricorn flowers

AQUARIUS AND PISCES
Dreamy and romantic Pisceans will intrigue you. Piscean charm will win your heart and bring out your protective instincts. This has the potential to be an extremely happy romance.

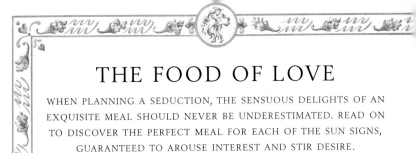

THE FOOD OF LOVE

WHEN PLANNING A SEDUCTION, THE SENSUOUS DELIGHTS OF AN
EXQUISITE MEAL SHOULD NEVER BE UNDERESTIMATED. READ ON
TO DISCOVER THE PERFECT MEAL FOR EACH OF THE SUN SIGNS,
GUARANTEED TO AROUSE INTEREST AND STIR DESIRE.

*Aquarians
will delight
in the subtle
and creamy
flavor and
light texture of
watercress soup.*

- THE FOOD OF LOVE -

FOR ARIENS
Spicy mulligatawny soup
·
Peppered steak
·
Baked Alaska

FOR TAUREANS
Cream of cauliflower soup
·
Tournedos Rossini
·
Rich chocolate and brandy mousse

FOR GEMINIANS
Seafood and avocado salad
·
Piquant stir-fried pork with ginger
·
Zabaglione

FOR CANCERIANS
Artichoke vinaigrette
·
Sole Bonne Femme
·
Almond soufflé

– THE FOOD OF LOVE –

FOR LEOS
Roasted tomato and garlic soup
·
Boeuf Stroganoff
·
Pears cooked in wine

FOR VIRGOS
Eggplant salad
·
Paella
·
French apple tart

FOR LIBRANS
Asparagus with hollandaise sauce
·
Pork with roasted apples
·
Strawberry Pavlova

FOR SCORPIOS
Vichyssoise
·
Lobster Newburg
·
Blueberry cream

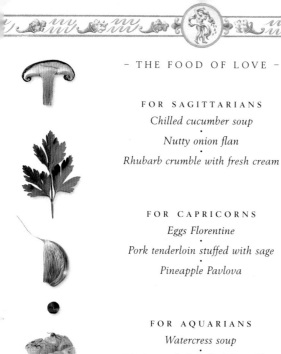

– THE FOOD OF LOVE –

FOR SAGITTARIANS
Chilled cucumber soup
·
Nutty onion flan
·
Rhubarb crumble with fresh cream

FOR CAPRICORNS
Eggs Florentine
·
Pork tenderloin stuffed with sage
·
Pineapple Pavlova

FOR AQUARIANS
Watercress soup
·
Chicken cooked with chili and lime
·
Lemon soufflé

FOR PISCEANS
French onion soup
·
Trout au vin rosé
·
Melon sorbet

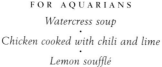

PLACES TO LOVE

ONCE YOU HAVE WON YOUR LOVER'S HEART, A ROMANTIC
VACATION TOGETHER WILL SEAL YOUR LOVE. HERE, YOU
CAN DISCOVER THE PERFECT DESTINATION FOR EACH SUN
SIGN, FROM HISTORIC CITIES TO IDYLLIC BEACHES.

THE
EIFFEL
TOWER,
PARIS

ARIES

*Florence is an Arien
city, and its perfectly
preserved Renaissance
palaces and churches
will set the scene for
wonderful romance.*

GEMINI

*Vivacious and restless
Geminians will feel at
home in the fast-paced
and sophisticated
atmosphere of
New York.*

TAURUS

*The unspoiled scenery
and unhurried pace
of life in rural Ireland
is sure to appeal to
patient and placid
Taureans.*

CANCER

*The watery beauty
and uniquely romantic
atmosphere of Venice
is guaranteed to arouse
passion and stir the
Cancerian imagination.*

ST. BASIL'S
CATHEDRAL,
MOSCOW

AYERS ROCK/ULURU,
AUSTRALIA

LEO
Leos will fall in love all over again when surrounded by the picturesque charm and unspoiled medieval atmosphere of Prague.

VIRGO
Perhaps the most elegant and romantic of all cities, Paris is certainly the ideal setting for a stylish and fastidious Virgo.

LIBRA
The dramatic and exotic beauty of Upper Egypt and the Nile will provide the perfect backdrop for wooing a romantic Libran.

SCORPIO
Intense and passionate Scorpios will be strongly attracted by the whiff of danger present in the exotic atmosphere of New Orleans.

SAGITTARIUS
The wide-ranging spaces of the Australian outback will appeal to the Sagittarian love of freedom and the great outdoors.

CAPRICORN
Capricorns will be fascinated and inspired by the great historical monuments of Moscow, the most powerful of all Russian cities.

AQUARIUS
Intrepid Aquarians will be enthralled and amazed by the unusual sights and spectacular landscapes of the Indian subcontinent.

PISCES
Water-loving Pisceans will be at their most relaxed and romantic by the sea, perhaps on a small and unspoiled Mediterranean island.

THE PYRAMIDS, EGYPT

GONDOLAS, VENICE

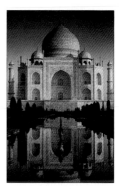

THE TAJ MAHAL, INDIA

VENUS & MARS

LUCID, SHINING VENUS AND FIERY, RED MARS HAVE ALWAYS BEEN
ASSOCIATED WITH HUMAN LOVE AND PASSION. THE TWO
PLANETS HAVE A POWERFUL INFLUENCE ON OUR ATTITUDES
TOWARD LOVE, SEX, AND RELATIONSHIPS.

The study of astrology first began long before humankind began to record its own history. The earliest astrological artifacts discovered, scratches on bones recording the phases of the Moon, date from well before the invention of any alphabet or writing system.

The planets Venus and Mars have always been regarded as having enormous significance in astrology. This is evident from the tentative attempts of early astrologers to record the effects of the two planets on humankind. Hundreds of years later, the positions of the planets were carefully noted in personal horoscopes. The earliest known record is dated 410 BC: "Venus [was] in the Bull, and Mars in the Twins."

The bright, shining planet Venus represents the gentle effect of the soul on our physical lives. It is responsible for a refined and romantic sensuality – "pure" love, untainted by sex. Venus reigns over our attitudes toward romance and the spiritual dimension of love.

The planet Mars affects the physical aspects of our lives – our strength, both physical and mental; our endurance; and our ability to fight for survival. Mars is also strongly linked to the sex drive of both men and women. Mars governs our physical energy, sexuality, and levels of desire.

Venus is known as an "inferior" planet, because its orbit falls between Earth and the Sun. Venus orbits the Sun

LOVE CONQUERS ALL

In Botticelli's Venus and Mars, *the warlike, fiery
energy of Mars, the god of war, has been overcome by
the gentle charms of Venus, the goddess of love.*

closely, and its position in the
zodiac is always in a sign near
that of the Sun. As a result, the
planet can only have occupied
one of five given signs at the
time of your birth – your Sun
sign, or the two signs before or
after it. For example, if you were
born with the Sun in Virgo,
Venus can only have occupied
Cancer, Leo, Virgo, Libra, or
Scorpio at that moment.

Mars, on the other hand, is
a "superior" planet. Its orbit lies
on the other side of Earth from

the Sun, and therefore the
planet may have occupied any
of the 12 signs at the moment
of your birth.

On the following pages
(24–45) we provide you with
fascinating insights into how
Mars and Venus govern your
attitudes toward love, sex, and
relationships. To ascertain which
sign of the zodiac the planets
occupied at the moment of
your birth, you must first consult
the tables on pages 52–61. Then
turn to page 24 and read on.

YOUR LOVE LIFE

THE PLANET VENUS REPRESENTS LOVE, HARMONY, AND UNITY.
WORK OUT WHICH SIGN OF THE ZODIAC VENUS OCCUPIED AT
THE MOMENT OF YOUR BIRTH (SEE PAGES 52–57), AND READ ON.

VENUS IN SAGITTARIUS

*T*hose born with Venus in Sagittarius tend to be independent both in thought and action. As an Aquarian, you can empathize with this characteristic; you are the individualist of the zodiac, and value your privacy highly.

For Aquarians, this planetary placing can be a very beneficial one. Sagittarius is a fire sign, and will give a welcome injection of warmth and passion to your cool Aquarian personality. You are likely to possess a broad romantic streak, and will throw yourself eagerly and wholeheartedly into a relationship. However, when it comes to making a serious commitment, you may feel intimidated by the prospect of a long-term relationship.

Intimacy is not a natural state for detached and self-sufficient Aquarians, and the freedom-loving influence of Sagittarius will not afford you much help in this area. However deeply in love you are, the prospect of having to change your habits and make compromises will not appeal to you.

Although Aquarians are not naturally disloyal or deceitful, Sagittarius is not renowned for its fidelity, and from this sign Venus could encourage you towards unfaithfulness and deception. You may even find that you allow these less attractive Sagittarian traits free rein in order to prevent yourself from becoming tied down in a permanent relationship.

You are staunchly loyal, and will go to great lengths to help your friends. However, like many Aquarians, you will be always be wary of any attempted invasion of your privacy. You tend to keep your own counsel and could find it difficult to open up, even to your closest confidants. Luckily, the good-humored and cheerful influence of Sagittarius should render you more approachable than the majority of Aquarians.

From this planetary placing, Venus will bring you a dose of emotional dynamism, and your courtship will be romantic and surprisingly ardent. You will always retain an aura of Aquarian remoteness, but your relationships will be conducted with vigor and in an open atmosphere. You are a considerate and stimulating lover, and your partner will find life with you rewarding and absorbing.

VENUS IN CAPRICORN

*T*he influence of Venus from Capricorn can be a trifle cooling. If Venus occupied this sign at the moment of your birth, you may be even more detached and unemotional than your fellow Aquarians. However, you will not suffer a shortage of admirers, for your powers of attraction are likely to be much more magnetic than usual.

Despite your popularity, you may find that you are reluctant to commit yourself to a permanent relationship, fearing the loss of your privacy and an invasion of your solitude. Do not take this attitude to extremes or allow it to prevent you from forming a very happy partnership. Even if you do not feel ready for an intense relationship or long-term commitment, there is no reason for you to reject every admirer as a matter of course and to miss out on all the fun and pleasure of a romantic affair.

Underneath their air of cool detachment, Aquarians are true romantics, but the prudent and calculating influence of Venus in Capricorn may subdue this attractive characteristic. Do not allow this placing of Venus to inhibit you. Your charming sentimental streak is one of your most attractive attributes, so allow yourself to succumb to your romantic urges and do not fend them off too vigorously.

Capricorn is a cautious influence, and Aquarius is often wary of making a commitment; therefore, you will be circumspect when it comes to entering into a relationship. However, when you do fall in love, you will fall heavily, and will be a fond and devoted partner. You will open yourself entirely to your lover, keeping nothing back whatsoever, and a rewarding and stimulating relationship should ensue. Once you take the plunge and decide

to make a serious commitment to your lover, you will not look back, and will prove an entirely loyal and constant partner. You will trust your lover implicitly, but if this trust is ever betrayed, you may be so disillusioned and disenchanted that forgiveness will be impossible.

Aquarians often labor under a delusion that once they have pledged their love, their partner will accept this as proof of their affections forever after, and will require no further reassurance. In reality, this is rarely the case. Most people continue to demand some visible assurance of their partner's continuing affections. Aquarians tend to be very self-sufficient and independent by nature; therefore, your partner may require regular demonstrations of your devotion as reassurance that your love is as strong and enduring as ever.

VENUS IN AQUARIUS

*W*hen Venus and the Sun occupy Aquarius at the same time, the planet will increase your need for independence; you may feel apprehensive at the prospect of entering into a relationship and sacrificing your freedom. However, you are likely to possess irresistible powers of attraction, and your cool and aloof aura will only make you more enigmatic and enticing. You will revel in the adoration and admiration of prospective partners, but if a potential friend or lover tries to come too close and break down your barriers, you will immediately draw back.

Your reluctance to become seriously involved in a long-term relationship does not mean that you are cold or self-centered. Aquarians are very sociable and greatly enjoy the company of others. You will be in great demand in a social situation, because you are stimulating and entertaining company. Once you have made friends, they will be your friends for life, and you will prove intensely loyal. However, if someone makes it evident that they hope to form a closer relationship with you, you will instinctively erect an impenetrable blockade to prevent an unwelcome intrusion into your private emotions. You tend to prefer group activities, because they are less intense than one-to-one relationships.

Do not allow your natural reluctance to sacrifice your privacy to prevent you from forming a happy and fulfilling partnership. When you meet someone you are attracted to, do not repress your feelings because you fear the loss of independence. Instead, try to explain to your potential lover how much you need your personal space. Perhaps you will

be pleasantly surprised – your potential partner might even be willing for you to retain a measure of independence within your relationship.

Aquarians are often very progressive, and are particularly attracted to unusual and unorthodox thinkers with non-conformist opinions. Try not to become too unconventional, or your potential partners may be put off by your eccentricity.

You are an Aquarian to the very core, and the intangible but irresistible air of romance and glamour which every Aquarian exudes to some extent will be yours in abundance. From this sign, Venus will boost your sexuality, and if you can open up and reveal your sensuality to your lover, your air of dreamy detachment and remoteness might not seem so threatening to your partner.

VENUS IN PISCES

*A*quarians tend to possess a strong romantic and sentimental streak, and these delightful qualities are underlined when Venus shines from Pisces. This planetary placing underlines your humanitarian instincts, charitable impulses, and natural kindness. As a result, you will be a responsive and warm lover, and appear much more approachable and open than many of your fellow Aquarians.

The Piscean influence is extremely poetic and emotional; when Venus occupies this sign, the planet will infuse your personality with these beguiling qualities. Your attitude may even occasionally verge on the sentimental, although your emotions will always be honestly and spontaneously expressed. Your underlying fear of losing your independence will abate, and you will find the prospect of a serious relationship less

intimidating than many Aquarians. You may still be prone to feelings of anxiety about losing your freedom and privacy, but you are less likely to become obsessed by your fear. Although you may have to struggle to overcome your anxiety and allow someone into your life, the powerful emotions of Pisces will eventually triumph. When you meet an attractive potential partner, a torrent of Piscean passion is likely to overcome any lingering Aquarian coolness and detachment.

Once you have taken the plunge and made a serious commitment, you will be among the most devoted, constant, and supportive of lovers. You will throw yourself into an alliance without a backward glance, and will work long and hard to ensure that it is a success. Try not to become too starry-eyed and idealistic about your emotional

relationship. You tend to be very sensitive and will find it difficult to cope with any form of infidelity.

Pisceans are sometimes prey to feelings of inadequacy and self-doubt; when Venus shines from Pisces you may find yourself doubting your abilities and questioning your powers of attraction. Do not underestimate your charms – your lack of confidence is entirely irrational.

Try to resist the temptation to take the easy way out of difficult situations. This Piscean habit can eventually lead to an atmosphere of confusion and deception infiltrating your relationship.

If you can diminish the effect of these minor negative traits, your Aquarian sympathy and understanding should combine with Piscean thoughtfulness and charm to make you a genuine, tender, and charming lover.

VENUS IN ARIES

*F*rom Aries, Venus will bring you a dash of energy and passion that will add fire to your rather cool Aquarian personality. You are likely to have a warmer nature than many Aquarians, and will be less detached and self-sufficient.

Aquarians value their solitude highly and tend to believe that a serious romantic commitment could threaten their treasured privacy. Although people born under this sign are friendly and sociable to everyone they meet, if they feel that their emotional space is being invaded they will immediately recoil.

However, when Venus shines from Aries, you will be far more open and demonstrative than many of your fellow Aquarians. Aquarian reticence will be replaced by Arien impulsiveness, and an exuberant and bold romantic streak will reveal itself in your personality. You are

likely to find that the warmth of Arien passion easily overpowers your natural Aquarian coolness and love of independence. Rather than withdrawing when a prospective partner makes it obvious that he or she finds you attractive, you are likely to seize the opportunity to pursue your admirer with true Arien ardor and determination. Try to cultivate these attractive traits and encourage them to flourish.

Venus from Aries is likely to bring you a welcome breath of energy and dynamism, but there is a danger that the planet will also bring a hint of Arien selfishness and impatience. When combined with the Aquarian disinclination to sacrifice your independence, any selfish streak could make you reluctant to compromise and could even threaten your relationships. You must consider the question of involvement

calmly and rationally. If you are able to explain your worries to your potential partner, your need for privacy is likely to be understood; you might even have considerable freedom.

You have a gregarious and friendly side to your personality and will blossom in social situations. Aquarians tend to be extremely loyal and constant friends, and once you establish a bond with someone, it will be a bond for life. Due to the Arien influence, you will be an inspiring companion, full of enthusiastic suggestions for mutual enjoyment and entertainment.

From Aries, Venus will imbue you with a seductive aura of romance. If you find a partner who will allow you plenty of space and time to yourself, your happiness will be infectious, and your lover will share your contentment with life.

YOUR SEX LIFE

THE PLANET MARS REPRESENTS PHYSICAL AND SEXUAL ENERGY.
WORK OUT WHICH SIGN OF THE ZODIAC MARS OCCUPIED AT THE
MOMENT OF YOUR BIRTH (SEE PAGES 58–61), AND READ ON.

MARS IN ARIES

*T*he fiery influence of Aries will endow you with plenty of physical stamina, and your lovemaking is likely to be energetic and passionate.

You will make a delightfully straightforward and genuine lover, and should be more open about your emotions than many Aquarians. Although you may be given to the occasional burst of temper, any sudden storms should soon blow over.

From Aries, Mars can bring a liking for freedom. This quality is also very typical of Aquarians; therefore, you must be aware of your need for independence, particularly when considering making a serious commitment.

MARS IN TAURUS

Taurean warmth will counter the characteristic coolness of the Aquarian lover, making you an affectionate and tender partner with considerable sexual stamina. Although Mars in Taurus is generally considered a helpful influence, there is a danger that this placing could make you possessive.

Mars in Taurus may bring you a dash of impatience and a hot temper. Your anger may flare up unexpectedly, but it will subside again just as swiftly.

However, when you lose your temper, you can express yourself very forcefully, sometimes with stronger language than the situation warrants. Make sure that your explosions do not intimidate your lover.

Aquarians tend to be unconventional and adventurous, but the influence of Taurus may increase your need for stability and routine. Try not to become obsessive about adhering to your daily schedule, or you may find yourself getting into a rut.

MARS IN GEMINI

*R*ather than boosting your physical energy, Mars in Gemini will emphasize your mental energy. Although you are likely to be an extremely imaginative and adventurous lover with a healthy sex drive, you will want to devote hours to thought-provoking discussions and debates with your partner.

You will possess plenty of physical energy and affection, and your sex life will be active and inventive, but there will be no deep streak of passion.

From Gemini, Mars may prove a rather flighty influence, and the planet will not be able to offer any help when it comes to your Aquarian fear of commitment. You may flit from lover to lover, and in this way manage to avoid making a serious involvement that could jeopardize your independence.

Due to the influence of Gemini, you may be tempted by the idea of infidelity, a quality that is entirely uncharacteristic of loyal and constant Aquarians.

MARS IN CANCER

*E*motional and sensual are the words which best describe the influence of Mars in Cancer. You will find it easy to express yourself, both physically and emotionally. As a result, you will be a sensual, affectionate, and imaginative lover.

When Mars shines from this sign, many intrinsic Aquarian qualities will be tempered by the influence of Cancer. The typical Aquarian air of detachment will be entirely missing from your personality. There is even a slight possibility that you may become rather clinging – a quality that is extremely uncharacteristic of a freedom-loving Aquarian.

Due to the influence of Mars in Cancer, a secure domestic environment will be one of your main aims in life. You will be eager to form a partnership, and may feel that a home and family are necessary to make your life complete. Do not allow your yearning for domestic bliss to persuade you to compromise in your choice of lover.

MARS IN LEO

Aquarian sensuality will be greatly boosted by the energetic and warmblooded sexual charisma of Leo, and you will be one of the most warm, passionate, and unselfish of lovers.

When Mars shines from Leo, your Aquarian glamor and appeal will be greatly enhanced. Your appearance may be more dramatic than usual, and your personality more colorful and beguiling. There is no danger that you will suffer from a lack of potential lovers and partners.

Indeed, you may even find that you have a superfluity of admirers, if this is possible.

Although you may retain a hint of Aquarian coolness, when Mars occupies Leo you will be energetic and enthusiastic when it comes to relationships. Leonine fieriness will overpower your fear of commitment, and you may even find yourself taking the lead in romantic situations. However, resist any leonine temptation to become dictatorial and domineering.

MARS IN VIRGO

The passion of Mars is lessened when it occupies Virgo; therefore, you may not be the most energetic of lovers. Do not allow any Virgoan reserve to inhibit your Aquarian sensuality.

If you can subdue a tendency toward modesty, you will discover that you possess a tender and earthy sexuality, which will be greatly enhanced by the imaginative and sensual powers of Aquarius. From Virgo, Mars may bring you a tendency to suffer from stress and nervous tension, but you should find that regular sex will dispel such ailments very effectively.

Aquarians can forget that their lover may occasionally need emotional reassurance, and unfortunately the natural reserve and diffidence of Virgo is unlikely to help in this area. Even if you are not naturally affectionate or demonstrative, you must enable your partner to feel confident and secure about the depth of your feelings and personal commitment.

MARS IN LIBRA

When Mars is placed in Libra, it will give your libido a boost. However, although the planet will increase your interest in sex, it will also reduce your physical energy. As a result, there is a danger that the relaxed Libran influence may combine with Aquarian coolness to make you a little too languid and laid-back, particularly when it comes to lovemaking.

However, once you have summoned up the energy to make love, you will be an irresistibly tender and gentle lover, and your partner will revel in your affectionate lovemaking.

The gentle influence of Libra may make you long for a secure and harmonious permanent relationship – an aim that will conflict with your Aquarian love of freedom. If you allow the generous and loving aspects of Libra to temper your fear of losing your independence, you should be able to form a happy and fulfilling relationship and enjoy a stimulating sex life.

MARS IN SCORPIO

*F*rom Scorpio, Mars will bring you a potent and vigorous sexuality, and you must channel it positively to ensure that you are sexually fulfilled. A romantic relationship that does not revolve around an active and imaginative sex life is unlikely to be successful.

Your vigor and energy should make you irresistible, and you will swiftly seduce anyone you set your sights on. If you can find a lover with a similarly high sex drive who also matches you in terms of sexual enthusiasm and inventiveness, you will make a wonderful partner. The only shadow that might hang over your relationship is your tendency towards jealousy. Try to control this dangerous emotion, or it may threaten your alliance.

When Mars shines from mysterious Scorpio, your natural Aquarian air of detachment may manifest itself as secretiveness. Be open with your partner – secrecy and concealment may alienate you from each other.

MARS IN SAGITTARIUS

*Y*our partner must share your sense of fun and high sex drive if you are to create a strong foundation for your relationship. You possess an abundance of enthusiasm and energy, which must be positively expressed to prevent you from becoming restless. Due to the Sagittarian influence, you detest monotony and tend to become easily bored. As a result, your lover will have to work very hard to prevent you from becoming tired of your relationship.

Aquarians are free spirits and are perhaps the most original and individual personalities in the zodiac. From Sagittarius, Mars may emphasize this trait and may even make you appear eccentric. Do not give your idiosyncrasies free rein, and avoid attempts to shock more conventional types with your outrageous behavior.

Due to the fiery, dynamic Sagittarian influence, you will be a passionate, vigorous, and exuberant lover.

MARS IN CAPRICORN

*M*ars is very well placed in Capricorn, giving you the ability to pace yourself well and to regulate your physical and mental energy. You are likely to be ambitious, with a strong will to succeed. Success in love will be just as important to you as success in your career.

Your emotional temperature will not be high, but this does not mean that you do not enjoy sex. You are a skilled and ardent lover, and revel in physical contact. Aquarians with Mars in Capricorn tend to have a strong sex drive, and your lovemaking will be sensual and energetic. You can give the impression of being cool and distant; therefore, you must remember to show some warmth and passion.

Make sure that your burning Capricorn ambition does not persuade you to channel your energy into your career rather than your relationship. If this happens, both the physical and emotional sides of your relationship may suffer.

MARS IN AQUARIUS

When both Mars and the Sun shine from Aquarius, all the qualities characteristic of the sign will be emphasized – in particular your need for freedom and independence.

You will find brief affairs very pleasurable, because you greatly enjoy sex and revel in imaginative lovemaking. However, if your lover suggests putting your affair on a more permanent footing, your immediate instinct will be to flee, even if you feel very much in love.

A perceptive lover may realize how much you value your independence, and might be persuaded to allow you the freedom you yearn for. This may sound like an ideal solution. However, complete freedom in a relationship is a difficult concept for many people, so think carefully before agreeing to such an arrangement. Your lover may not be the jealous type, but is likely to discover that the idea of an open relationship is one thing and the reality another.

MARS IN PISCES

*T*he romantic side of the Aquarian character is strongly emphasized by Mars in Pisces. At first you may appear rather remote, but soon your lover will realize that beneath your cool exterior runs a deep vein of emotion.

You are very sensual, and possess a vivid and passionate sexuality. This will not be expressed with great physical vigor, but through a leisurely, deliberate eroticism that will leave your partner weak with desire. Do not be embarrassed by your strong Piscean passions. Take pleasure in your sensuality, and when you get carried away enjoy the sensation without feeling guilty.

Due to the Piscean influence, you may lack self-confidence. You must instill a sense of your own value in yourself and should not underestimate your abilities. Concentrate on showing yourself in your true colors – a truly sympathetic, creative, and passionate lover.

TOKENS OF LOVE

ASTROLOGY CAN GIVE YOU A FASCINATING INSIGHT INTO YOUR
LOVER'S PERSONALITY AND ATTITUDE TOWARD LOVE. IT CAN
ALSO PROVIDE YOU WITH SOME INVALUABLE HINTS WHEN YOU
WANT TO CHOOSE THE PERFECT GIFT FOR YOUR LOVER.

ARIES

*Sports equipment will
please an active Arien.
Instead of chocolates,
give your Arien lover a
box of crystallized ginger.*

GOLF TEES

CRYSTALLIZED
GINGER

TAURUS

*An elegant home
environment is of
great importance to
Taureans, and your
Taurean lover will
be delighted by a
plump, luxurious
tapestry cushion.*

TAPESTRY
CUSHION

CARVED
AGATE
PORTRAIT

GEMINI

*Any items made from
agate will be greatly
treasured because it is
the Geminian stone.*

BRASS BIRD
CURIO

CANCER

*Cancerians adore
unusual curios and love
collecting antiques.
A domesticated
Cancerian will also
welcome a cook
book or a selection of
unusual foods.*

DRIED CHILIES AND
ORNAMENTAL PASTA

INDIAN
PERFUME
BOTTLE

WILDFLOWER
HONEY

GOLDEN CROWN
CANDLEHOLDER

CRYSTALLIZED
FRUITS

LEO

*A bottle of perfume or
aftershave will delight your
Leo lover. Gold is the Leo
metal, therefore anything
gold or gold-colored will
also make a perfect gift.*

VIRGO

*Instead of chocolates,
give your health-
conscious Virgoan
lover a special jar
of honey or a box of
crystallized fruits.*

– TOKENS OF LOVE –

VIOLIN

SCENTED
BATH OIL

DECORATIVE
TOOTHBRUSH

LIBRA
*Librans are true
romantics. They
enjoy all types
of music and will
adore any recordings
of their favorite
classical pieces.*

SCORPIO
*Decorative
bathroom products
and accessories
will always be
enjoyed by your
Scorpio lover
because Scorpio
is a water sign.*

VICTORIAN
TRAVEL BOOKS

SAGITTARIUS
*Adventurous and
independent Sagittarians
love to travel. Any travel
books or accessories, such as
maps or compasses, will be greatly
appreciated by a Sagittarian lover.*

IVY

SILVER
PICTURE
FRAME

CAPRICORN

*Only the best will do for a
fastidious Capricorn. If
you would like to buy your
lover a plant, choose ivy. A
silver picture frame will also
enchant a Capricorn.*

BUTTERFLY
BROOCH

AQUARIUS

*Glittery pieces of
costume jewelry
will charm an
Aquarian.*

GIVING A BIRTHSTONE

AQUAMARINE

*The most personal
gift you can give
your lover is the
gem linked to his
or her Sun sign.*

ARIES: *diamond*
TAURUS: *emerald*
GEMINI: *agate* · CANCER: *pearl*
LEO: *ruby* · VIRGO: *sardonyx*
LIBRA: *sapphire* · SCORPIO: *opal*
SAGITTARIUS: *topaz*
CAPRICORN: *amethyst*
AQUARIUS: *aquamarine*
PISCES: *moonstone*

THAI
SILK
SCARF

PISCES

*A soft and
sumptuous
silk scarf will
delight a sensual
Piscean. Iridescent
glass will also
please a Piscean lover.*

IRIDESCENT
GLASS
MARBLES

YOUR PERMANENT RELATIONSHIP

AQUARIANS MAKE KIND AND CONSIDERATE LOVERS. HOWEVER,
THEIR NEED FOR SOLITUDE AND PRIVACY MAY MAKE IT DIFFICULT
FOR THEM TO SETTLE INTO A PERMANENT RELATIONSHIP.

*A*quarians can find it very difficult to enter into and sustain a close emotional relationship. This is mainly due to your determination to protect your personal space. Your fear of intrusion can be so strong that it may keep you single all your life, or prevent you from committing yourself until you are well into middle age.

People who fall for an Aquarian will have to realize from the very beginning that they are not going to be treated to frequent and lavish displays of love and affection. If you find yourself having to provide constant reassurance of your affection, your lover has chosen the wrong person. Aquarians tend to assume that having

pledged themselves to a partner, no more proof of their devotion should be demanded of them.

However, for many people this apparent lack of emotion is unsatisfactory, and your lover may demand more overt declarations of affection. Encourage the elements of romance in your personality to grow and flourish, and allow them to invigorate and animate your relationship.

Aquarians are intensely private people, and will always need to retain a degree of privacy. Make sure that your lover is aware of your need for solitude from the start of your relationship. It will help if you have chosen someone who will not be offended or dismayed by

A JOINT FUTURE

On a Sailing Ship, by Caspar David Friedrich, shows a newly married couple sailing into a bright but unknown future together.

the fact that there are hidden depths to your personality, known to you alone. If this idea is hard for your lover to come to terms with, some difficulties may arise in a long-term relationship.

Despite your need for seclusion, life with you can be a great pleasure, for you are kind, considerate, and encouraging, and help your lover toward fulfillment. You will welcome signs of your partner's success and individuality, and you expect that your partner will be equally pleased for you in your shining moments.

When you fall in love, you will be totally loyal and faithful to the person you have chosen. If you can both manage to come to terms with the idiosyncratic Aquarian lifestyle, an exciting, rewarding, and entirely fulfilling partnership will follow.

VENUS & MARS TABLES

THESE TABLES WILL ENABLE YOU TO DISCOVER WHICH SIGNS
VENUS AND MARS OCCUPIED AT THE MOMENT OF YOUR BIRTH.
TURN TO PAGES 24–45 TO INVESTIGATE THE QUALITIES OF THESE
SIGNS, AND TO FIND OUT HOW THEY WORK WITH YOUR SUN SIGN.

*T*he tables on pages 53–61 will enable you to discover the positions of Venus and Mars at the moment of your birth.

First find your year of birth on the top line of the appropriate table, then find your month of birth in the left-hand column. Where the column for your year of birth intersects with the row for your month of birth, you will find a group of figures and zodiacal glyphs. These figures and glyphs show which sign of the zodiac the planet occupied

on the first day of that month, and any date during that month on which the planet moved into another sign.

For example, to ascertain the position of Venus on May 10, 1968, run your finger down the column marked 1968 until you reach the row for May. The row of numbers and glyphs shows that Venus occupied Aries on May 1, entered Taurus on May 4, and then moved into Gemini on May 28. Therefore, on May 10, Venus was in Taurus.

If you were born on a day when one of the planets was moving into a new sign, it may be impossible to determine your Venus and Mars signs completely accurately. If the characteristics described on the relevant pages do not seem to apply to you, read the interpretation of the sign before and after. One of these signs will be appropriate.

ZODIACAL GLYPHS

♈	Aries	♎	Libra
♉	Taurus	♏	Scorpio
♊	Gemini	♐	Sagittarius
♋	Cancer	♑	Capricorn
♌	Leo	♒	Aquarius
♍	Virgo	♓	Pisces

♀	1921	1922	1923	1924	1925	1926	1927	1928
JAN	1 ♒ 7 ♓	1 ♑ 25 ♒	1 ♏ 3 ♐	1 ♒ 20 ♓	1 ♐ 15 ♑	1 ♒	1 ♑ 10 ♒	1 ♏ 5 ♐ 30 ♑
FEB	1 ♓ 3 ♈	1 ♒ 18 ♓	1 ♐ 7 ♑ 14 ♒	1 ♓ 14 ♈	1 ♑ 8 ♒	1 ♒	1 ♒ 3 ♓ 27 ♈	1 ♑ 23 ♒
MAR	1 ♈ 8 ♉	1 ♓ 14 ♈	1 ♒	1 ♈ 10 ♉	1 ♒ 5 ♓ 29 ♈	1 ♒	1 ♈ 23 ♉	1 ♒ 19 ♓
APR	1 ♉ 26 ♈	1 ♈ 7 ♉	1 ♒ 2 ♓ 27 ♈	1 ♉ 8 ♊	1 ♈ 22 ♉	1 ♒ 22 ♓	1 ♉ 17 ♊	1 ♓ 12 ♈
MAY	1 ♈	1 ♉ 2 ♊ 26 ♋	1 ♈ 22 ♉	1 ♊ 7 ♋	1 ♉ 16 ♊	1 ♓ 7 ♈	1 ♊ 13 ♋	1 ♈ 7 ♉ 31 ♊
JUN	1 ♈ 3 ♉	1 ♋ 20 ♌	1 ♉ 16 ♊	1 ♋	1 ♊ 10 ♋	1 ♈ 3 ♉ 29 ♊	1 ♋ 9 ♌	1 ♊ 24 ♋
JUL	1 ♉ 9 ♊	1 ♌ 16 ♍	1 ♊ 11 ♋	1 ♋	1 ♋ 4 ♌ 29 ♍	1 ♊ 25 ♋	1 ♌ 8 ♍	1 ♋ 19 ♌
AUG	1 ♊ 6 ♋	1 ♍ 11 ♎	1 ♋ 4 ♌ 28 ♍	1 ♋	1 ♍ 23 ♎	1 ♋ 19 ♌	1 ♍	1 ♌ 12 ♍
SEP	1 ♌ 27 ♍	1 ♎ 8 ♏	1 ♍ 22 ♎	1 ♋ 8 ♌	1 ♎ 17 ♏	1 ♌ 12 ♍	1 ♍	1 ♍ 5 ♎ 30 ♏
OCT	1 ♍ 21 ♎	1 ♏ 11 ♐	1 ♎ 16 ♏	1 ♌ 8 ♍	1 ♏ 12 ♐	1 ♍ 6 ♎ 30 ♏	1 ♍	1 ♏ 24 ♐
NOV	1 ♎ 14 ♏	1 ♐ 29 ♏	1 ♏ 9 ♐	1 ♍ 3 ♎ 28 ♏	1 ♐ 7 ♑	1 ♏ 23 ♐	1 ♍ 10 ♎	1 ♐ 18 ♑
DEC	1 ♏ 8 ♐	1 ♏	1 ♐ 3 ♑ 27 ♒	1 ♏ 22 ♐	1 ♑ 6 ♒	1 ♐ 17 ♑	1 ♎ 9 ♏	1 ♑ 13 ♒

♀	1929	1930	1931	1932	1933	1934	1935	1936
JAN	1 ♒ 7 ♓	1 ♑ 25 ♒	1 ♏ 4 ♐	1 ♒ 20 ♓	1 ♐ 15 ♑	1 ♒	1 ♑ 9 ♒	1 ♏ 4 ♐ 29 ♑
FEB	1 ♓ 3 ♈	1 ♒ 17 ♓	1 ♐ 7 ♑	1 ♓ 13 ♈	1 ♑ 8 ♒	1 ♒	1 ♒ 2 ♓ 27 ♈	1 ♑ 23 ♒
MAR	1 ♈ 9 ♉	1 ♓ 13 ♈	1 ♑ 6 ♒	1 ♈ 10 ♉	1 ♒ 4 ♓ 28 ♈	1 ♒	1 ♈ 23 ♉	1 ♒ 18 ♓
APR	1 ♉ 21 ♈	1 ♈ 7 ♉	1 ♓ 27 ♈	1 ♉ 6 ♊	1 ♈ 21 ♉	1 ♒ 22 ♓	1 ♉ 17 ♊	1 ♓ 12 ♈
MAY	1 ♈	1 ♉ 2 ♊ 26 ♋	1 ♈ 22 ♉	1 ♊ 7 ♋	1 ♉ 16 ♊	1 ♓ 7 ♈	1 ♊ 12 ♋	1 ♈ 6 ♉ 30 ♊
JUN	1 ♈ 4 ♉	1 ♋ 20 ♌	1 ♉ 15 ♊	1 ♋	1 ♊ 9 ♋	1 ♈ 3 ♉ 29 ♊	1 ♋ 8 ♌	1 ♊ 24 ♋
JUL	1 ♉ 9 ♊	1 ♌ 15 ♍	1 ♊ 10 ♋	1 ♋ 14 ♊ 29 ♋	1 ♋ 4 ♌ 28 ♍	1 ♊ 24 ♋	1 ♌ 8 ♍	1 ♋ 18 ♌
AUG	1 ♊ 6 ♋	1 ♍ 11 ♎	1 ♋ 4 ♌ 28 ♍	1 ♋	1 ♍ 22 ♎	1 ♋ 18 ♌	1 ♍	1 ♌ 12 ♍
SEP	1 ♌ 26 ♍	1 ♎ 8 ♏	1 ♍ 21 ♎	1 ♋ 9 ♌	1 ♎ 16 ♏	1 ♌ 12 ♍	1 ♍	1 ♍ 5 ♎ 29 ♏
OCT	1 ♍ 21 ♎	1 ♏ 13 ♐	1 ♎ 15 ♏	1 ♌ 8 ♍	1 ♏ 12 ♐	1 ♍ 6 ♎ 30 ♏	1 ♍	1 ♏ 24 ♐
NOV	1 ♎ 14 ♏	1 ♐ 23 ♏	1 ♏ 8 ♐	1 ♍ 3 ♎ 28 ♏	1 ♐ 7 ♑	1 ♏ 23 ♐	1 ♍ 10 ♎	1 ♐ 17 ♑
DEC	1 ♏ 8 ♐ 31 ♑	1 ♏	1 ♐ 2 ♑ 26 ♒	1 ♏ 22 ♐	1 ♑ 6 ♒	1 ♐ 17 ♑	1 ♎ 9 ♏	1 ♑ 12 ♒

♀	1937	1938	1939	1940	1941	1942	1943	1944
JAN	1♒ 7♓	1♑ 24♒	1♏ 5♐	1♒ 19♓	1♐ 14♑	1♒	1♑ 9♒	1♏ 4♐ 29♑
FEB	1♓ 3♈	1♒ 17♓	1♐ 7♑	1♓ 13♈	1♑ 7♒	1♒	1♒ 2♓ 26♈	1♑ 22♒
MAR	1♈ 10♉	1♓ 13♈	1♑ 6♒	1♈ 9♉	1♒ 3♓ 28♈	1♒	1♈ 22♉	1♒ 18♓
APR	1♉ 15♈	1♈ 6♉ 30♊	1♓ 26♈	1♉	1♈ 21♉	1♒ 7♓	1♉ 16♊	1♓ 11♈
MAY	1♈	1♊ 25♋	1♈ 21♉	1♉ 7♊	1♉ 15♊	1♓ 7♈	1♊ 12♋	1♈ 5♉ 30♊
JUN	1♈ 5♉	1♋ 19♌	1♉ 15♊	1♋	1♊ 8♋	1♈ 3♉ 28♊	1♋ 8♌	1♊ 23♋
JUL	1♉ 8♊	1♌ 15♍	1♊ 10♋	1♋ 6♊	1♋ 3♌ 28♍	1♊ 24♋	1♌ 8♍	1♋ 18♌
AUG	1♊ 5♋	1♍ 10♎	1♋ 3♌ 27♍	1♊ 2♋	1♍ 22♎	1♋ 18♌	1♍	1♌ 11♍
SEP	1♌ 26♍	1♎ 8♏	1♍ 21♎	1♋ 9♌	1♎ 16♏	1♌ 11♍	1♍	1♍ 4♎ 29♏
OCT	1♍ 20♎	1♏ 14♐	1♎ 15♏	1♌ 15♍	1♏ 11♐	1♍ 5♎ 29♏	1♍	1♏ 23♐
NOV	1♎ 13♏	1♐ 16♏	1♏ 8♐	1♍ 8♎	1♐ 7♑	1♏ 22♐	1♍ 22♎	1♐ 17♑
DEC	1♏ 7♐ 31♑	1♏	1♐ 2♑ 26♒	1♎ 2♏ 27♐	1♑ 6♒	1♐ 16♑	1♎ 9♏	1♑ 12♒

♀	1945	1946	1947	1948	1949	1950	1951	1952
JAN	1♒ 6♓	1♑ 23♒	1♏ 6♐	1♒ 19♓	1♐ 14♑	1♒	1♑ 8♒	1♏ 3♐ 28♑
FEB	1♓ 3♈	1♒ 16♓	1♐ 7♑	1♓ 12♈	1♑ 7♒	1♒	1♒ 2♓ 25♈	1♑ 21♒
MAR	1♈ 12♉	1♓ 12♈	1♑ 6♒ 31♓	1♈ 9♉	1♒ 3♓ 27♈	1♒	1♈ 22♉	1♒ 17♓
APR	1♉ 8♈	1♈ 6♉ 30♊	1♓ 24♈	1♉	1♈ 20♉	1♒ 6♓	1♉ 16♊	1♓ 10♈
MAY	1♈	1♊ 25♋	1♈ 21♉	1♉ 8♊	1♉ 15♊	1♓ 6♈	1♊ 12♋	1♈ 5♉ 29♊
JUN	1♈ 5♉	1♋ 19♌	1♉ 14♊	1♋ 30♊	1♊ 8♋	1♈ 2♉ 28♊	1♋ 8♌	1♊ 22♋
JUL	1♉ 8♊	1♌ 14♍	1♊ 9♋	1♊	1♋ 2♌ 27♍	1♊ 23♋	1♌ 8♍	1♋ 17♌
AUG	1♊ 5♋ 31♌	1♍ 10♎	1♋ 3♌ 27♍	1♊ 4♋	1♍ 21♎	1♋ 17♌	1♍	1♌ 10♍
SEP	1♌ 25♍	1♎ 8♏	1♍ 20♎	1♋ 9♌	1♎ 15♏	1♌ 11♍	1♍	1♍ 4♎ 28♏
OCT	1♍ 20♎	1♏ 17♐	1♎ 14♏	1♌ 12♍	1♏ 11♐	1♍ 5♎ 29♏	1♍	1♏ 23♐
NOV	1♎ 13♏	1♐ 9♏	1♏ 7♐	1♍ 5♎ 30♏	1♐ 7♑	1♏ 22♐	1♍ 22♎	1♐ 16♑
DEC	1♏ 7♐ 31♑	1♏	1♑ 25♒	1♏ 24♐	1♑ 7♒	1♐ 15♑	1♎ 9♏	1♑ 11♒

♀	1953	1954	1955	1956	1957	1958	1959	1960
JAN	1 ♒ 6 ♓	1 ♑ 23 ♒	1 ♏ 7 ♐	1 ♒ 18 ♓	1 ♐ 13 ♑	1 ♒	1 ♑ 8 ♒	1 ♏ 3 ♐ 28 ♑
FEB	1 ♓ 3 ♈	1 ♒ 16 ♓	1 ♐ 7 ♑	1 ♓ 12 ♈	1 ♑ 6 ♒	1 ♒	1 ♓ 25 ♈	1 ♑ 21 ♒
MAR	1 ♈ 15 ♉	1 ♓ 12 ♈	1 ♑ 5 ♒ 31 ♓	1 ♈ 8 ♉	1 ♒ 2 ♓ 26 ♈	1 ♒	1 ♈ 21 ♉	1 ♒ 16 ♓
APR	1 ♈	1 ♈ 5 ♉ 29 ♊	1 ♓ 25 ♈	1 ♉ 5 ♊	1 ♈ 19 ♉	1 ♒ 7 ♓	1 ♉ 15 ♊	1 ♓ 10 ♈
MAY	1 ♈	1 ♊ 24 ♉	1 ♈ 20 ♉	1 ♉ 9 ♊	1 ♉ 14 ♊	1 ♓ 6 ♈	1 ♊ 11 ♋	1 ♈ 4 ♉ 29 ♊
JUN	1 ♈ 6 ♉	1 ♋ 18 ♌	1 ♉ 14 ♊	1 ♋ 24 ♊	1 ♊ 7 ♋	1 ♈ 2 ♉ 27 ♊	1 ♋ 7 ♌	1 ♊ 22 ♋
JUL	1 ♉ 8 ♊	1 ♌ 14 ♍	1 ♊ 14 ♋	1 ♊	1 ♋ 2 ♌ 27 ♍	1 ♊ 22 ♋	1 ♌ 9 ♍	1 ♋ 16 ♌
AUG	1 ♊ 5 ♋ 31 ♌	1 ♍ 10 ♎	1 ♋ 2 ♌ 26 ♍	1 ♊ 5 ♋	1 ♍ 21 ♎	1 ♋ 16 ♌	1 ♍	1 ♌ 9 ♍
SEP	1 ♌ 25 ♍	1 ♎ 7 ♏	1 ♍ 19 ♎	1 ♋ 9 ♌	1 ♎ 15 ♏	1 ♌ 10 ♍	1 ♍ 21 ♌ 26 ♍	1 ♍ 3 ♎ 28 ♏
OCT	1 ♍ 19 ♎	1 ♏ 24 ♐ 28 ♏	1 ♎ 13 ♏	1 ♌ 7 ♍	1 ♏ 11 ♐	1 ♍ 3 ♎ 28 ♏	1 ♍	1 ♏ 22 ♐
NOV	1 ♎ 12 ♏	1 ♏	1 ♏ 6 ♐	1 ♎ 26 ♏	1 ♐ 6 ♑	1 ♏ 21 ♐	1 ♍ 10 ♎	1 ♐ 16 ♑
DEC	1 ♏ 6 ♐ 30 ♑	1 ♏	1 ♑ 25 ♒	1 ♏ 20 ♐	1 ♑ 7 ♒	1 ♐ 15 ♑	1 ♎ 8 ♏	1 ♑ 11 ♒

♀	1961	1962	1963	1964	1965	1966	1967	1968
JAN	1 ♒ 6 ♓	1 ♑ 22 ♒	1 ♏ 7 ♐	1 ♒ 17 ♓	1 ♐ 13 ♑	1 ♒	1 ♑ 7 ♒ 31 ♓	1 ♏ 2 ♐ 27 ♑
FEB	1 ♓ 3 ♈	1 ♒ 15 ♓	1 ♐ 6 ♑	1 ♓ 11 ♈	1 ♑ 6 ♒	1 ♒ 7 ♓ 26 ♒	1 ♓ 24 ♈	1 ♑ 21 ♒
MAR	1 ♈	1 ♓ 11 ♈	1 ♑ 5 ♒ 31 ♓	1 ♈ 8 ♉	1 ♒ 2 ♓ 26 ♈	1 ♒	1 ♈ 21 ♉	1 ♒ 16 ♓
APR	1 ♈	1 ♈ 4 ♉ 29 ♊	1 ♓ 25 ♈	1 ♉ 5 ♊	1 ♈ 19 ♉	1 ♒ 7 ♓	1 ♉ 15 ♊	1 ♓ 9 ♈
MAY	1 ♈	1 ♊ 24 ♉	1 ♈ 19 ♉	1 ♉ 10 ♊	1 ♉ 13 ♊	1 ♓ 6 ♈	1 ♊ 11 ♋	1 ♈ 4 ♉ 28 ♊
JUN	1 ♈ 6 ♉	1 ♋ 18 ♌	1 ♉ 13 ♊	1 ♋ 18 ♊	1 ♊ 7 ♋	1 ♉ 27 ♊	1 ♊ 7 ♋	1 ♊ 21 ♋
JUL	1 ♉ 8 ♊	1 ♌ 13 ♍	1 ♊ 8 ♋	1 ♊	1 ♌ 26 ♍	1 ♊ 22 ♋	1 ♌ 9 ♍	1 ♋ 16 ♌
AUG	1 ♊ 4 ♋ 30 ♌	1 ♍ 9 ♎	1 ♌ 26 ♍	1 ♊ 6 ♋	1 ♍ 20 ♎	1 ♋ 16 ♌	1 ♍	1 ♌ 9 ♍
SEP	1 ♌ 24 ♍	1 ♎ 8 ♏	1 ♍ 18 ♎	1 ♋ 9 ♌	1 ♎ 14 ♏	1 ♌ 9 ♍	1 ♍ 10 ♎	1 ♍ 3 ♎ 27 ♏
OCT	1 ♍ 18 ♎	1 ♏	1 ♎ 13 ♏	1 ♌ 6 ♍	1 ♏ 10 ♐	1 ♍ 3 ♎ 27 ♏	1 ♌ 2 ♍	1 ♏ 22 ♐
NOV	1 ♎ 12 ♏	1 ♏	1 ♏ 6 ♐ 30 ♑	1 ♎ 25 ♏	1 ♐ 6 ♑	1 ♏ 20 ♐	1 ♍ 10 ♎	1 ♐ 15 ♑
DEC	1 ♏ 6 ♐ 29 ♑	1 ♏	1 ♑ 24 ♒	1 ♏ 20 ♐	1 ♑ 8 ♒	1 ♐ 14 ♑	1 ♎ 8 ♏	1 ♑ 10 ♒

♀	1969	1970	1971	1972	1973	1974	1975	1976
JAN	1 ♒ 5 ♓	1 ♑ 22 ♒	1 ♏ 8 ♐	1 ♒ 17 ♓	1 ♐ 12 ♑	1 ♒ 30 ♑	1 ♑ 7 ♒ 31 ♓	1 ♏ 2 ♐ 27 ♑
FEB	1 ♓ 3 ♈	1 ♒ 15 ♓	1 ♐ 6 ♑	1 ♓ 5 ♈	1 ♑ 5 ♒	1 ♑	1 ♓ 24 ♈	1 ♑ 20 ♒
MAR	1 ♈	1 ♓ 11 ♈	1 ♑ 5 ♒ 30 ♓	1 ♓ 8 ♈	1 ♓ 25 ♈	1 ♒	1 ♈ 20 ♉	1 ♒ 15 ♓
APR	1 ♈	1 ♈ 4 ♉ 28 ♊	1 ♓ 24 ♈	1 ♈ 4 ♉	1 ♈ 19 ♉	1 ♒ 7 ♓	1 ♉ 14 ♊	1 ♓ 9 ♈
MAY	1 ♈	1 ♊ 23 ♋	1 ♈ 19 ♉	1 ♉ 11 ♊	1 ♉ 13 ♊	1 ♓ 5 ♈	1 ♊ 10 ♋	1 ♈ 3 ♉ 27 ♊
JUN	1 ♈ 6 ♉	1 ♋ 17 ♌	1 ♉ 13 ♊	1 ♊ 12 ♋	1 ♉ 6 ♊	1 ♈ 26 ♉	1 ♋ 7 ♌	1 ♊ 21 ♋
JUL	1 ♉ 13 ♊	1 ♌ 13 ♍	1 ♊ 7 ♋	1 ♊	1 ♊	1 ♉ 26 ♊	1 ♊ 10 ♋	1 ♋ 15 ♌
AUG	1 ♊ 4 ♋ 30 ♌	1 ♍ 9 ♎	1 ♋ 25 ♌	1 ♊ 7 ♋	1 ♍ 19 ♎	1 ♋ 15 ♌	1 ♍	1 ♌ 9 ♍
SEP	1 ♌ 24 ♍	1 ♎	1 ♍ 18 ♎	1 ♋ 8 ♌	1 ♌ 14 ♍	1 ♌ 9 ♍	1 ♌ 3 ♍	1 ♍ 2 ♎ 26 ♏
OCT	1 ♍ 18 ♎	1 ♏	1 ♎ 12 ♏	1 ♌ 5 ♍ 31 ♎	1 ♍ 10 ♎	1 ♏	1 ♌ 5 ♍	1 ♏ 21 ♐
NOV	1 ♎ 11 ♏	1 ♏	1 ♏ 5 ♐ 30 ♑	1 ♎ 25 ♏	1 ♏ 6 ♐	1 ♏ 20 ♐	1 ♍ 10 ♎	1 ♐ 15 ♑
DEC	1 ♏ 5 ♐ 29 ♑	1 ♏	1 ♑ 24 ♒	1 ♏ 19 ♐	1 ♐ 8 ♑	1 ♐ 14 ♑	1 ♎ 7 ♏	1 ♑ 10 ♒

♀	1977	1978	1979	1980	1981	1982	1983	1984
JAN	1 ♒ 5 ♓	1 ♑ 21 ♒	1 ♏ 8 ♐	1 ♒ 16 ♓	1 ♐ 12 ♑	1 ♒ 24 ♑	1 ♑ 6 ♒ 30 ♓	1 ♏ 2 ♐ 26 ♑
FEB	1 ♓ 3 ♈	1 ♒ 14 ♓	1 ♐ 6 ♑	1 ♓ 10 ♈	1 ♑ 5 ♒ 28 ♓	1 ♑	1 ♓ 23 ♈	1 ♑ 20 ♒
MAR	1 ♈	1 ♓ 10 ♈	1 ♒ 4 ♓ 29 ♈	1 ♓ 7 ♈	1 ♓ 25 ♈	1 ♑ 3 ♒	1 ♈ 20 ♉	1 ♒ 15 ♓
APR	1 ♈	1 ♈ 3 ♉ 28 ♊	1 ♓ 23 ♈	1 ♈ 4 ♉	1 ♈ 18 ♉	1 ♒ 7 ♓	1 ♉ 14 ♊	1 ♓ 8 ♈
MAY	1 ♈	1 ♊ 22 ♋	1 ♈ 18 ♉	1 ♉ 13 ♊	1 ♉ 12 ♊	1 ♓ 5 ♈	1 ♊ 10 ♋	1 ♈ 3 ♉ 27 ♊
JUN	1 ♈ 7 ♉	1 ♋ 17 ♌	1 ♉ 12 ♊	1 ♊ 6 ♋ 30 ♌	1 ♉ 6 ♊	1 ♈ 26 ♉	1 ♋ 7 ♌	1 ♊ 21 ♋
JUL	1 ♉ 12 ♊	1 ♌ 12 ♍	1 ♊ 7 ♋ 31 ♌	1 ♊	1 ♌ 25 ♍	1 ♊ 21 ♋	1 ♌ 11 ♍	1 ♋ 15 ♌
AUG	1 ♊ 3 ♋ 29 ♌	1 ♍ 8 ♎	1 ♌ 18 ♍	1 ♊ 7 ♋	1 ♍ 19 ♎	1 ♋ 15 ♌	1 ♍ 28 ♌	1 ♋ 8 ♍
SEP	1 ♌ 23 ♍	1 ♎ 8 ♏	1 ♍ 18 ♎	1 ♌ 8 ♍	1 ♍ 13 ♎	1 ♌ 8 ♍	1 ♌	1 ♍ 2 ♎ 26 ♏
OCT	1 ♍ 17 ♎	1 ♏	1 ♎ 12 ♏	1 ♌ 5 ♍ 31 ♎	1 ♍ 9 ♎	1 ♌ 2 ♍ 26 ♎	1 ♌ 6 ♍	1 ♏ 21 ♐
NOV	1 ♎ 11 ♏	1 ♏	1 ♏ 5 ♐ 29 ♑	1 ♎ 25 ♏	1 ♏ 6 ♐	1 ♏ 19 ♐	1 ♍ 10 ♎	1 ♐ 14 ♑
DEC	1 ♏ 4 ♐ 28 ♑	1 ♏	1 ♑ 23 ♒	1 ♏ 19 ♐	1 ♐ 9 ♑	1 ♐ 12 ♑	1 ♎ 7 ♏	1 ♑ 10 ♒

♀	1985	1986	1987	1988	1989	1990	1991	1992
JAN	1 ♒ 5 ♓	1 ♑ 21 ♒	1 ♏ 8 ♐	1 ♒ 16 ♓	1 ♐ 11 ♑	1 ♒ 17 ♑	1 ♑ 6 ♒ 30 ♓	1 ♐ 26 ♑
FEB	1 ♓ 3 ♈	1 ♒ 14 ♓	1 ♐ 6 ♑	1 ♓ 10 ♈	1 ♑ 4 ♒ 28 ♓	1 ♑	1 ♓ 23 ♈	1 ♑ 19 ♒
MAR	1 ♈	1 ♓ 9 ♈	1 ♑ 4 ♒ 29 ♓	1 ♈ 7 ♉	1 ♓ 24 ♈	1 ♑ 4 ♒	1 ♈ 19 ♉	1 ♒ 14 ♓
APR	1 ♈	1 ♈ 3 ♉ 27 ♊	1 ♓ 23 ♈	1 ♉ 3 ♊	1 ♈ 17 ♉	1 ♒ 7 ♓	1 ♉ 13 ♊	1 ♓ 7 ♈
MAY	1 ♈	1 ♊ 22 ♋	1 ♈ 18 ♉	1 ♊ 18 ♋ 27 ♊	1 ♉ 12 ♊	1 ♓ 4 ♈ 31 ♉	1 ♊ 9 ♋	1 ♈ 2 ♉ 26 ♊
JUN	1 ♈ 7 ♉	1 ♋ 16 ♌	1 ♉ 12 ♊	1 ♊	1 ♊ 5 ♋ 30 ♌	1 ♉ 25 ♊	1 ♋ 7 ♌	1 ♊ 20 ♋
JUL	1 ♉ 7 ♊	1 ♌ 12 ♍	1 ♊ 6 ♋ 31 ♌	1 ♊	1 ♌ 24 ♍	1 ♊ 20 ♋	1 ♌ 11 ♍	1 ♋ 14 ♌
AUG	1 ♊ 3 ♋ 28 ♌	1 ♍ 8 ♎	1 ♌ 24 ♍	1 ♊ 7 ♋	1 ♍ 18 ♎	1 ♋ 13 ♌	1 ♍ 22 ♌	1 ♌ 7 ♍
SEP	1 ♌ 23 ♍	1 ♏	1 ♍ 17 ♎	1 ♋ 8 ♌	1 ♎ 13 ♏	1 ♌ 9 ♍	1 ♌	1 ♍ 25 ♎
OCT	1 ♍ 17 ♎	1 ♏	1 ♎ 11 ♏	1 ♌ 5 ♍ 30 ♎	1 ♏ 9 ♐	1 ♍ 2 ♎ 26 ♏	1 ♌ 7 ♍	1 ♎ 20 ♏
NOV	1 ♎ 10 ♏	1 ♏	1 ♏ 4 ♐ 28 ♑	1 ♎ 24 ♏	1 ♐ 6 ♑	1 ♏ 19 ♐	1 ♍ 19 ♎	1 ♏ 14 ♐
DEC	1 ♏ 4 ♐ 28 ♑	1 ♏	1 ♑ 23 ♒	1 ♏ 18 ♐	1 ♑ 10 ♒	1 ♐ 13 ♑	1 ♎ 7 ♏	1 ♐ 9 ♑

♀	1993	1994	1995	1996	1997	1998	1999	2000
JAN	1 ♒ 4 ♓	1 ♑ 20 ♒	1 ♏ 8 ♐	1 ♒ 15 ♓	1 ♐ 10 ♑	1 ♒ 10 ♑	1 ♑ 5 ♒ 29 ♓	1 ♐ 25 ♑
FEB	1 ♓ 3 ♈	1 ♒ 13 ♓	1 ♐ 5 ♑	1 ♓ 9 ♈	1 ♑ 4 ♒ 28 ♓	1 ♑	1 ♓ 22 ♈	1 ♑ 19 ♒
MAR	1 ♈	1 ♓ 9 ♈	1 ♑ 3 ♒ 29 ♓	1 ♈ 6 ♉	1 ♓ 24 ♈	1 ♑ 5 ♒	1 ♈ 19 ♉	1 ♒ 14 ♓
APR	1 ♈	1 ♈ 2 ♉ 27 ♊	1 ♓ 23 ♈	1 ♉ 4 ♊	1 ♈ 17 ♉	1 ♒ 7 ♓	1 ♉ 13 ♊	1 ♓ 7 ♈
MAY	1 ♈	1 ♊ 21 ♋	1 ♈ 17 ♉	1 ♊	1 ♉ 11 ♊	1 ♓ 4 ♈ 30 ♉	1 ♊ 9 ♋	1 ♈ 2 ♉ 26 ♊
JUN	1 ♈ 7 ♉	1 ♋ 15 ♌	1 ♉ 11 ♊	1 ♊	1 ♊ 4 ♋ 29 ♌	1 ♉ 25 ♊	1 ♋ 6 ♌	1 ♊ 19 ♋
JUL	1 ♉ 6 ♊	1 ♌ 12 ♍	1 ♊ 6 ♋ 30 ♌	1 ♊	1 ♌ 24 ♍	1 ♊ 20 ♋	1 ♌ 13 ♍	1 ♋ 13 ♌
AUG	1 ♊ 2 ♋ 28 ♌	1 ♍ 8 ♎	1 ♌ 23 ♍	1 ♊ 8 ♋	1 ♍ 14 ♎	1 ♋ 14 ♌	1 ♍ 16 ♌	1 ♌ 7 ♍
SEP	1 ♌ 22 ♍	1 ♎ 8 ♏	1 ♍ 17 ♎	1 ♋ 8 ♌	1 ♎ 12 ♏	1 ♌ 7 ♍	1 ♌	1 ♍ 25 ♎
OCT	1 ♍ 16 ♎	1 ♏	1 ♎ 11 ♏	1 ♌ 5 ♍ 30 ♎	1 ♏ 9 ♐	1 ♎ 23 ♏	1 ♌ 8 ♍	1 ♎ 20 ♏
NOV	1 ♎ 9 ♏	1 ♏	1 ♏ 4 ♐ 28 ♑	1 ♎ 23 ♏	1 ♐ 6 ♑	1 ♏ 18 ♐	1 ♍ 10 ♎	1 ♏ 13 ♐
DEC	1 ♏ 3 ♐ 27 ♑	1 ♏	1 ♑ 22 ♒	1 ♏ 17 ♐	1 ♑ 12 ♒	1 ♐ 12 ♑	1 ♎ 6 ♏	1 ♐ 9 ♑

♂	1921	1922	1923	1924	1925	1926	1927	1928	1929	1930
JAN	1 ♒ 5 ♓	1 ♏	1 ♓ 21 ♈	1 ♏ 19 ♐	1 ♈	1 ♐	1 ♉	1 ♐ 19 ♑	1 ♊	1 ♑
FEB	1 ♓ 13 ♈	1 ♏ 18 ♐	1 ♈	1 ♐	1 ♈ 5 ♉	1 ♐ 9 ♑	1 ♉ 22 ♊	1 ♑ 28 ♒	1 ♊	1 ♑ 6 ♒
MAR	1 ♈ 25 ♉	1 ♐	1 ♈ 4 ♉	1 ♐ 6 ♑	1 ♉ 24 ♊	1 ♑ 23 ♒	1 ♊	1 ♒	1 ♊ 10 ♋	1 ♒ 17 ♓
APR	1 ♉	1 ♐	1 ♉ 16 ♊	1 ♑ 24 ♒	1 ♊	1 ♒	1 ♊ 17 ♋	1 ♒ 7 ♓	1 ♋	1 ♓ 24 ♈
MAY	1 ♉ 6 ♊	1 ♐	1 ♊ 30 ♋	1 ♒	1 ♊ 9 ♋	1 ♒ 3 ♓	1 ♋	1 ♓ 16 ♈	1 ♋ 13 ♌	1 ♈
JUN	1 ♊ 18 ♋	1 ♐	1 ♋	1 ♒ 24 ♓	1 ♋ 26 ♌	1 ♓ 15 ♈	1 ♋ 6 ♌	1 ♈ 26 ♉	1 ♌	1 ♈ 3 ♉
JUL	1 ♋	1 ♐	1 ♋ 16 ♌	1 ♓	1 ♌	1 ♈	1 ♌ 25 ♍	1 ♉	1 ♌ 4 ♍	1 ♉ 14 ♊
AUG	1 ♋ 3 ♌	1 ♐	1 ♌	1 ♓ 24 ♒	1 ♌ 12 ♍	1 ♉	1 ♍	1 ♉ 9 ♊	1 ♍ 21 ♎	1 ♊ 28 ♋
SEP	1 ♌ ♍	1 ♐ 13 ♑	1 ♍	1 ♒	1 ♍ 28 ♎	1 ♉	1 ♍ 10 ♎	1 ♊	1 ♎	1 ♋
OCT	1 ♍	1 ♑ 30 ♒	1 ♍ 18 ♎	1 ♒ 19 ♓	1 ♎	1 ♉	1 ♎ 26 ♏	1 ♊ 3 ♋	1 ♎ 6 ♏	1 ♋ 20 ♌
NOV	1 ♍ 6 ♎	1 ♒	1 ♎	1 ♓	1 ♎ 13 ♏	1 ♉	1 ♏	1 ♋	1 ♏ 18 ♐	1 ♌
DEC	1 ♎ 26 ♏	1 ♒ 11 ♓	1 ♎ 4 ♏	1 ♓ 19 ♈	1 ♏ 28 ♐	1 ♉	1 ♏ 8 ♐	1 ♋ 20 ♊	1 ♐ 29 ♑	1 ♌

♂	1931	1932	1933	1934	1935	1936	1937	1938	1939	1940
JAN	1 ♌	1 ♑ 18 ♒	1 ♍	1 ♒	1 ♎	1 ♒ 14 ♓	1 ♎ 5 ♏	1 ♓ 30 ♈	1 ♏ 29 ♐	1 ♓ 4 ♈
FEB	1 ♌ 16 ♋	1 ♒ 25 ♓	1 ♍	1 ♒ 4 ♓	1 ♎	1 ♓ 22 ♈	1 ♏	1 ♈	1 ♐	1 ♈ 17 ♉
MAR	1 ♋ 30 ♌	1 ♓	1 ♍	1 ♓ 14 ♈	1 ♎	1 ♈	1 ♏ 13 ♐	1 ♈ 12 ♉	1 ♐ 21 ♑	1 ♉
APR	1 ♌	1 ♓ 3 ♈	1 ♍	1 ♈ 22 ♉	1 ♎	1 ♉	1 ♐	1 ♉ 23 ♊	1 ♑	1 ♊
MAY	1 ♌	1 ♈ 12 ♉	1 ♍	1 ♉	1 ♎	1 ♉ 13 ♊	1 ♐ 14 ♏	1 ♊	1 ♑ 25 ♒	1 ♊ 17 ♋
JUN	1 ♌ 10 ♍	1 ♉ 22 ♊	1 ♍	1 ♉ 2 ♊	1 ♎	1 ♊ 25 ♋	1 ♏	1 ♊ 7 ♋	1 ♒	1 ♋
JUL	1 ♍	1 ♊	1 ♍ 6 ♎	1 ♊ 15 ♋	1 ♎ 29 ♏	1 ♋	1 ♏	1 ♋ 22 ♌	1 ♒ 21 ♑	1 ♋ 3 ♌
AUG	1 ♎	1 ♊ 4 ♋	1 ♎ 26 ♏	1 ♋ 30 ♌	1 ♏	1 ♋ 10 ♌	1 ♏ 8 ♐	1 ♌	1 ♑	1 ♌ 19 ♍
SEP	1 ♎ 17 ♏	1 ♋ 20 ♌	1 ♏	1 ♌	1 ♏ 16 ♐	1 ♌ 26 ♍	1 ♐ 30 ♑	1 ♌ 7 ♍	1 ♑ ♒	1 ♍
OCT	1 ♏ 30 ♐	1 ♌	1 ♏ 9 ♐	1 ♌ 18 ♍	1 ♐ 28 ♑	1 ♍	1 ♑	1 ♍ 25 ♎	1 ♒	1 ♍ 5 ♎
NOV	1 ♐	1 ♌ 13 ♍	1 ♐ 19 ♑	1 ♍	1 ♑	1 ♍ 14 ♎	1 ♑ 11 ♒	1 ♎	1 ♒ 19 ♓	1 ♎ 20 ♏
DEC	1 ♐ 10 ♑	1 ♍	1 ♑ 28 ♒	1 ♍ 11 ♎	1 ♑ 7 ♒	1 ♎	1 ♒ 21 ♓	1 ♎ 11 ♏	1 ♓	1 ♏

– MARS TABLES –

♂	1941	1942	1943	1944	1945	1946	1947	1948	1949	1950
JAN	1♏ 4♐	1♈ 11♉	1♐ 26♑	1♊	1♐ 5♑	1♋	1♑ 25♒	1♍	1♑ 4♒	1♎
FEB	1♐ 17♑	1♉	1♑	1♊	1♑ 14♒	1♋	1♒	1♍ 12♌	1♒ 11♓	1♎
MAR	1♑	1♉ 7♊	1♑ 8♒	1♊ 29♋	1♒ 25♓	1♋	1♒ 4♓	1♌	1♓ 21♈	1♎
APR	1♑ 2♒	1♊ 26♋	1♒ 17♓	1♋	1♓	1♋ 22♌	1♓ 11♈	1♌	1♈ 30♉	1♎
MAY	1♒ 16♓	1♋	1♓ 27♈	1♋ 22♌	1♓ 3♈	1♌	1♈ 21♉	1♌ 18♍	1♉	1♎
JUN	1♓	1♋ 14♌	1♈	1♌	1♈ 11♉	1♌ 20♍	1♉	1♍	1♉ 10♊	1♎
JUL	1♓ 2♈	1♌	1♈ 7♉	1♌ 12♍	1♉ 23♊	1♍	1♊	1♍ 17♎	1♊ 23♋	1♎
AUG	1♈	1♍	1♉ 23♊	1♍ 29♎	1♊	1♍ 9♎	1♊ 13♋	1♎	1♋	1♎ 10♏
SEP	1♈	1♍ 17♎	1♊	1♎	1♊ 7♋	1♎ 24♏	1♋	1♎ 3♏	1♋ 7♌	1♏ 25♐
OCT	1♈	1♎	1♊	1♎ 13♏	1♋	1♏	1♌	1♏ 17♐	1♌ 27♍	1♐
NOV	1♈	1♎ 2♏	1♊	1♏ 25♐	1♋ 11♌	1♏ 6♐	1♌	1♐ 26♑	1♍	1♐ 6♑
DEC	1♈	1♏ 15♐	1♊	1♐	1♌ 26♋	1♐ 17♑	1♍	1♑	1♍ 26♎	1♑ 15♒

♂	1951	1952	1953	1954	1955	1956	1957	1958	1959	1960
JAN	1♒ 22♓	1♎ 20♏	1♓	1♏	1♉ 15♊	1♑ 14♒	1♈ 28♉	1♐	1♊	1♑ 14♒
FEB	1♓	1♏	1♓ 8♈	1♏ 9♐	1♊ 26♋	1♒	1♉	1♐ 3♑	1♊ 10♋	1♒ 23♓
MAR	1♓ 2♈	1♏	1♈ 20♉	1♐	1♋	1♒	1♉ 17♊	1♑ 17♒	1♋	1♓
APR	1♈ 10♉	1♏	1♉	1♐ 12♑	1♋ 10♌	1♒	1♊	1♒ 27♓	1♋ 10♌	1♓ 2♈
MAY	1♉ 21♊	1♏	1♊	1♑	1♌ 26♍	1♒	1♊ 4♋	1♓	1♌	1♈ 11♉
JUN	1♊	1♏	1♊ 14♋	1♑	1♍	1♒	1♋ 21♌	1♓ 7♈	1♌ 1♍	1♉ 20♊
JUL	1♊ 3♋	1♏	1♋ 29♌	1♑ 3♒	1♍ 11♎	1♒	1♌	1♈ 21♉	1♍ 20♎	1♊
AUG	1♋ 18♌	1♏ 27♐	1♌	1♒ 24♓	1♎ 27♏	1♒ 14♓	1♌ 8♍	1♉	1♎	1♊
SEP	1♌	1♐	1♌ 14♍	1♓	1♏	1♓	1♍ 24♎	1♉ 21♊	1♎ 5♏	1♊ 21♋
OCT	1♌ 5♍	1♐ 12♑	1♍	1♓ 21♈	1♏ 13♐	1♓	1♎	1♊	1♏ 21♐	1♋
NOV	1♍ 24♎	1♑ 21♒	1♎	1♈	1♐ 29♑	1♓ 16♈	1♎ 8♏	1♊	1♐	1♋
DEC	1♎	1♒ 30♓	1♎ 20♏	1♈ 4♉	1♑	1♈	1♏ 23♐	1♊	1♐ 3♑	1♋

♂	1961	1962	1963	1964	1965	1966	1967	1968	1969	1970
JAN	1 ♋	1 ♑	1 ♌	1 ♑ 13 ♒	1 ♍	1 ♒ 30 ♓	1 ♎	1 ♒ 9 ♓	1 ♏	1 ♓ 24 ♈
FEB	1 ♋ 5 ♊ 7 ♋	1 ♑ 2 ♒	1 ♌	1 ♒ 20 ♓	1 ♍	1 ♓	1 ♎ 12 ♏	1 ♓ 17 ♈	1 ♏ 25 ♐	1 ♈
MAR	1 ♋	1 ♒ 12 ♓	1 ♌	1 ♓ 29 ♈	1 ♍	1 ♓ 9 ♈	1 ♏ 31 ♎	1 ♈ 28 ♉	1 ♐	1 ♈ 7 ♉
APR	1 ♋	1 ♓ 19 ♈	1 ♌	1 ♈	1 ♍	1 ♈ 17 ♉	1 ♎	1 ♉	1 ♐	1 ♉ 18 ♊
MAY	1 ♋ 6 ♌	1 ♈ 28 ♉	1 ♌	1 ♈ 7 ♉	1 ♍	1 ♉ 28 ♊	1 ♎	1 ♉ 8 ♊	1 ♐	1 ♊
JUN	1 ♌ 28 ♍	1 ♉	1 ♌ 3 ♍	1 ♉ 17 ♊	1 ♍ 29 ♎	1 ♊	1 ♎	1 ♊ 21 ♋	1 ♐	1 ♊ 2 ♋
JUL	1 ♍	1 ♉ 9 ♊	1 ♍ 27 ♎	1 ♊ 30 ♋	1 ♎	1 ♊ 11 ♋	1 ♎ 19 ♏	1 ♋	1 ♐	1 ♋ 18 ♌
AUG	1 ♍ 17 ♎	1 ♊ 22 ♋	1 ♎	1 ♋	1 ♎ 20 ♏	1 ♋ 25 ♌	1 ♏	1 ♋ 5 ♌	1 ♐	1 ♌
SEP	1 ♎	1 ♋	1 ♎ 12 ♏	1 ♋ 15 ♌	1 ♏	1 ♌	1 ♏ 10 ♐	1 ♌ 21 ♍	1 ♐ 21 ♑	1 ♌ 3 ♍
OCT	1 ♎ 2 ♏	1 ♋ 11 ♌	1 ♏ 25 ♐	1 ♌	1 ♏ 4 ♐	1 ♌ 12 ♍	1 ♐ 23 ♑	1 ♍	1 ♑	1 ♍ 20 ♎
NOV	1 ♏ 13 ♐	1 ♌	1 ♐	1 ♌ 6 ♍	1 ♐ 14 ♑	1 ♍	1 ♑	1 ♍ 9 ♎	1 ♑ 4 ♒	1 ♎
DEC	1 ♐ 24 ♑	1 ♌	1 ♐ 5 ♑	1 ♍	1 ♑ 23 ♒	1 ♍ 4 ♎	1 ♑ 2 ♒	1 ♎ 30 ♏	1 ♒ 15 ♓	1 ♎ 6 ♏

♂	1971	1972	1973	1974	1975	1976	1977	1978	1979	1980
JAN	1 ♏ 23 ♐	1 ♈	1 ♐	1 ♉	1 ♐ 21 ♑	1 ♊	1 ♑	1 ♌ 26 ♋	1 ♑ 21 ♒	1 ♍
FEB	1 ♐	1 ♈ 10 ♉	1 ♐ 12 ♑	1 ♉ 27 ♊	1 ♑	1 ♊	1 ♑ 9 ♒	1 ♋	1 ♒ 28 ♓	1 ♍
MAR	1 ♐ 12 ♑	1 ♉ 27 ♊	1 ♑ 27 ♒	1 ♊	1 ♑ 3 ♒	1 ♊ 18 ♋	1 ♒ 20 ♓	1 ♋	1 ♓	1 ♍ 12 ♌
APR	1 ♑	1 ♊	1 ♒	1 ♊ 20 ♋	1 ♒ 11 ♓	1 ♋	1 ♓ 28 ♈	1 ♋ 11 ♌	1 ♓ 7 ♈	1 ♌
MAY	1 ♑ 3 ♒	1 ♊ 12 ♋	1 ♒ 8 ♓	1 ♋	1 ♓ 21 ♈	1 ♋ 16 ♌	1 ♈	1 ♌	1 ♈ 16 ♉	1 ♌ 4 ♍
JUN	1 ♒	1 ♋ 28 ♌	1 ♓ 21 ♈	1 ♋ 9 ♌	1 ♈	1 ♌	1 ♈ 6 ♉	1 ♌ 14 ♍	1 ♉ 26 ♊	1 ♍
JUL	1 ♒	1 ♌	1 ♈	1 ♌ 27 ♍	1 ♉	1 ♌ 7 ♍	1 ♉ 18 ♊	1 ♍	1 ♊	1 ♍ 11 ♎
AUG	1 ♒	1 ♌ 15 ♍	1 ♈ 12 ♉	1 ♍	1 ♉ 14 ♊	1 ♍ 24 ♎	1 ♊	1 ♍ 4 ♎	1 ♊ 8 ♋	1 ♎ 29 ♏
SEP	1 ♒	1 ♍	1 ♉	1 ♍ 12 ♎	1 ♊	1 ♎	1 ♋	1 ♎ 20 ♏	1 ♋ 25 ♌	1 ♏
OCT	1 ♒	1 ♎	1 ♉ 30 ♈	1 ♎ 28 ♏	1 ♊ 17 ♋	1 ♎ 9 ♏	1 ♋ 27 ♌	1 ♏	1 ♌	1 ♏ 12 ♐
NOV	1 ♒ 6 ♓	1 ♎ 15 ♏	1 ♈	1 ♏	1 ♋ 26 ♊	1 ♏ 21 ♐	1 ♌	1 ♏ 2 ♐	1 ♌ 20 ♍	1 ♐ 22 ♑
DEC	1 ♓ 26 ♈	1 ♏ 30 ♐	1 ♈ 24 ♉	1 ♏ 11 ♐	1 ♊	1 ♐	1 ♌	1 ♐ 13 ♑	1 ♍	1 ♑ 31 ♒

– MARS TABLES –

♂	1981	1982	1983	1984	1985	1986	1987	1988	1989	1990
JAN	1 ♒	1 ♎	1 ♒ 17 ♓	1 ♎ 11 ♏	1 ♓	1 ♏	1 ♓ 8 ♈	1 ♏ 8 ♐	1 ♈ 19 ♉	1 ♐ 30 ♑
FEB	1 ♒ 7 ♓	1 ♎	1 ♓ 25 ♈	1 ♏	1 ♓ 3 ♈	1 ♏ 2 ♐	1 ♈ 21 ♉	1 ♐ 22 ♑	1 ♉	1 ♑
MAR	1 ♓ 17 ♈	1 ♎	1 ♈	1 ♏	1 ♈ 15 ♉	1 ♐ 28 ♑	1 ♉	1 ♑	1 ♉ 11 ♊	1 ♑ 12 ♒
APR	1 ♈ 25 ♉	1 ♎	1 ♈ 5 ♉	1 ♏	1 ♉ 26 ♊	1 ♑	1 ♉ 6 ♊	1 ♑ 6 ♒	1 ♊ 29 ♋	1 ♒ 21 ♓
MAY	1 ♉	1 ♎	1 ♉ 17 ♊	1 ♏	1 ♊	1 ♑	1 ♊ 21 ♋	1 ♒ 22 ♓	1 ♋	1 ♓ 31 ♈
JUN	1 ♉ 5 ♊	1 ♎	1 ♊ 29 ♋	1 ♏	1 ♊ 9 ♋	1 ♑	1 ♋	1 ♓	1 ♋ 17 ♌	1 ♈
JUL	1 ♊ 18 ♋	1 ♎	1 ♋	1 ♏	1 ♋ 25 ♌	1 ♑	1 ♋ 7 ♌	1 ♓ 14 ♈	1 ♌	1 ♈ 13 ♉
AUG	1 ♋	1 ♎ 3 ♏	1 ♋ 14 ♌	1 ♏ 18 ♐	1 ♌	1 ♑	1 ♌ 23 ♍	1 ♈	1 ♌ 3 ♍	1 ♉ 31 ♊
SEP	1 ♋ 2 ♌	1 ♏ 20 ♐	1 ♌ 30 ♍	1 ♐	1 ♌ 10 ♍	1 ♑	1 ♍	1 ♈	1 ♍ 20 ♎	1 ♊
OCT	1 ♌ 21 ♍	1 ♐	1 ♍	1 ♐ 5 ♑	1 ♍ 28 ♎	1 ♑ 9 ♒	1 ♍ 9 ♎	1 ♈	1 ♎	1 ♊
NOV	1 ♍	1 ♑	1 ♍ 18 ♎	1 ♑ 16 ♒	1 ♎	1 ♒ 26 ♓	1 ♎ 24 ♏	1 ♈	1 ♎ 4 ♏	1 ♊
DEC	1 ♍ 16 ♎	1 ♑ 10 ♒	1 ♎	1 ♒ 25 ♓	1 ♎ 15 ♏	1 ♓	1 ♏	1 ♈	1 ♏ 18 ♐	1 ♊ 14 ♉

♂	1991	1992	1993	1994	1995	1996	1997	1998	1999	2000
JAN	1 ♉ 21 ♊	1 ♐ 9 ♑	1 ♋	1 ♑ 28 ♒	1 ♍ 23 ♌	1 ♑ 9 ♒	1 ♍ 3 ♎	1 ♒ 25 ♓	1 ♎ 26 ♏	1 ♒ 4 ♓
FEB	1 ♊	1 ♑ 18 ♒	1 ♋	1 ♒	1 ♌	1 ♒ 15 ♓	1 ♎	1 ♓	1 ♏	1 ♓ 12 ♈
MAR	1 ♊	1 ♒ 28 ♓	1 ♋	1 ♒ 7 ♓	1 ♌	1 ♓ 25 ♈	1 ♎ 8 ♍	1 ♓ 5 ♈	1 ♏	1 ♈ 23 ♉
APR	1 ♊ 3 ♋	1 ♓	1 ♋ 28 ♌	1 ♓ 15 ♈	1 ♌	1 ♈	1 ♍	1 ♈ 13 ♉	1 ♏	1 ♉
MAY	1 ♋ 27 ♌	1 ♓ 6 ♈	1 ♌	1 ♈ 24 ♉	1 ♌ 26 ♍	1 ♈ 3 ♉	1 ♍	1 ♉ 24 ♊	1 ♏ 6 ♎	1 ♉ 4 ♊
JUN	1 ♌	1 ♈ 15 ♉	1 ♌ 23 ♍	1 ♉	1 ♍	1 ♉ 12 ♊	1 ♍ 19 ♎	1 ♊	1 ♎	1 ♊ 16 ♋
JUL	1 ♌ 16 ♍	1 ♉ 27 ♊	1 ♍	1 ♉ 4 ♊	1 ♍ 21 ♎	1 ♊ 26 ♋	1 ♎	1 ♊ 6 ♋	1 ♎ 5 ♏	1 ♋
AUG	1 ♍	1 ♊	1 ♍ 12 ♎	1 ♊ 17 ♋	1 ♎	1 ♋	1 ♎ 14 ♏	1 ♋ 21 ♌	1 ♏	1 ♌
SEP	1 ♎	1 ♊ 12 ♋	1 ♍ 27 ♎	1 ♋	1 ♎ 7 ♏	1 ♋ 10 ♌	1 ♏ 28 ♐	1 ♌	1 ♏ 3 ♐	1 ♌ 17 ♍
OCT	1 ♎ 17 ♏	1 ♋	1 ♏	1 ♋ 5 ♌	1 ♏ 20 ♐	1 ♌ 30 ♍	1 ♐	1 ♌ 7 ♍	1 ♐ 17 ♑	1 ♍
NOV	1 ♏ 29 ♐	1 ♋	1 ♏ 9 ♐	1 ♌	1 ♐ 30 ♑	1 ♍	1 ♐ 9 ♑	1 ♍ 27 ♎	1 ♑ 26 ♒	1 ♍ 4 ♎
DEC	1 ♐	1 ♋	1 ♐ 20 ♑	1 ♌ 12 ♍	1 ♑	1 ♍	1 ♑ 18 ♒	1 ♎	1 ♒	1 ♎ 23 ♏